MY FIVE SENSES

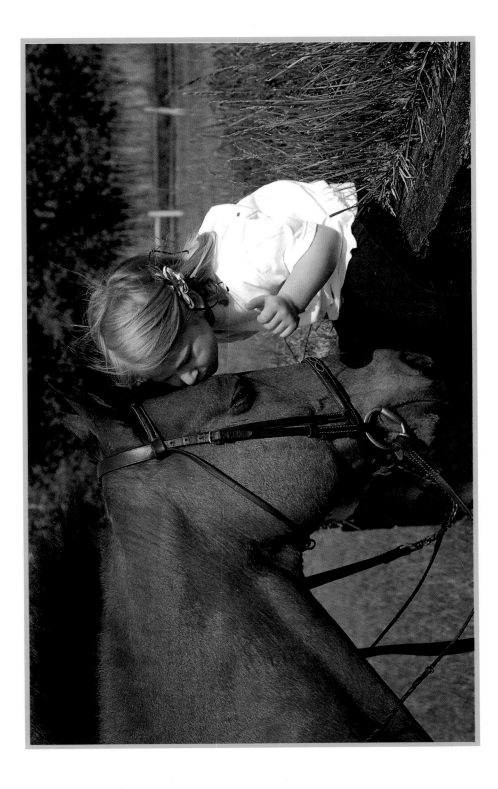

BY MARGARET MILLER

Aladdin Paperbacks

For my mother,
who always encouraged me to see

ACKNOWLEDGMENTS
My special thanks to the children in this book:
Miranda Berman, Annie Bernard, Rafael Espaillat,
Max and Gus Halper, Gideon Jacobs, and Morgan Means. —M. M.

First Aladdin Paperbacks edition July 1998

Aladdin Paperbacks
An imprint of Simon & Schuster Children's Publishing Division
1230 Avenue of the Americas
New York, NY 10020

Also available in a Simon & Schuster
Books for Young Readers hardcover edition.

Designed by Sylvia Frezzolini

Manufactured in China

20

The Library of Congress has cataloged the
hardcover edition as follows:

Miller, Margaret.
My five senses / by Margaret Miller.   p.   cm.
Summary: A simple introduction to the five senses
and how they help us experience the world around us.
ISBN 0-671-79168-0
1. Senses and sensation—Juvenile literature. [1. Senses and sensation.]
I. Title.
QP434.M55   1993   93-1956
612.8—dc20   CIP
ISBN 0-689-82009-7 (pbk.)
0311 SCP

I have two eyes, a nose,

a mouth, two ears, and two hands.

With my eyes I see myself,

my shadow,

my dog,

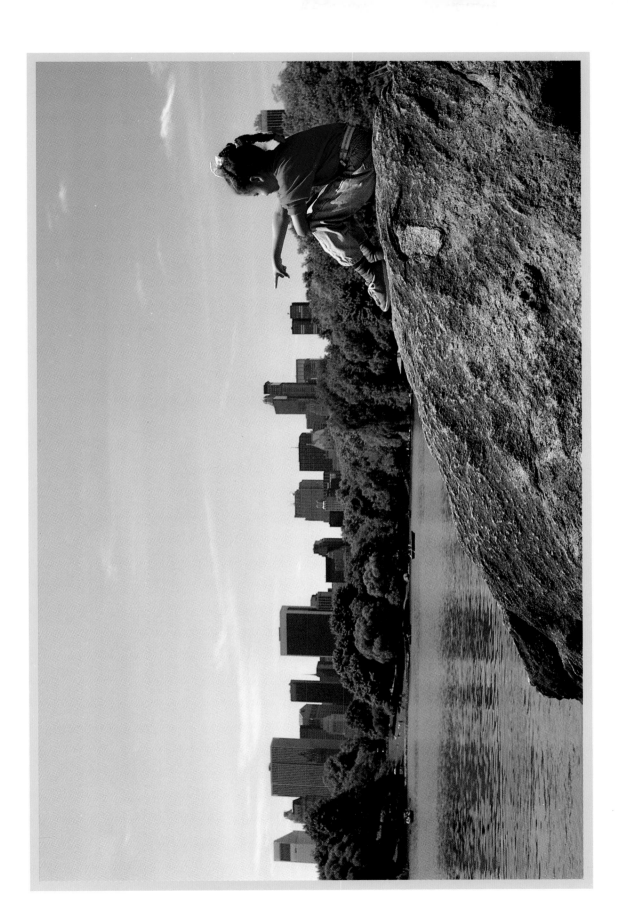

and my city.

With my nose I smell popcorn,

a horse,

flowers,

and garbage.

With my mouth I taste watermelon,

the ocean,

medicine,

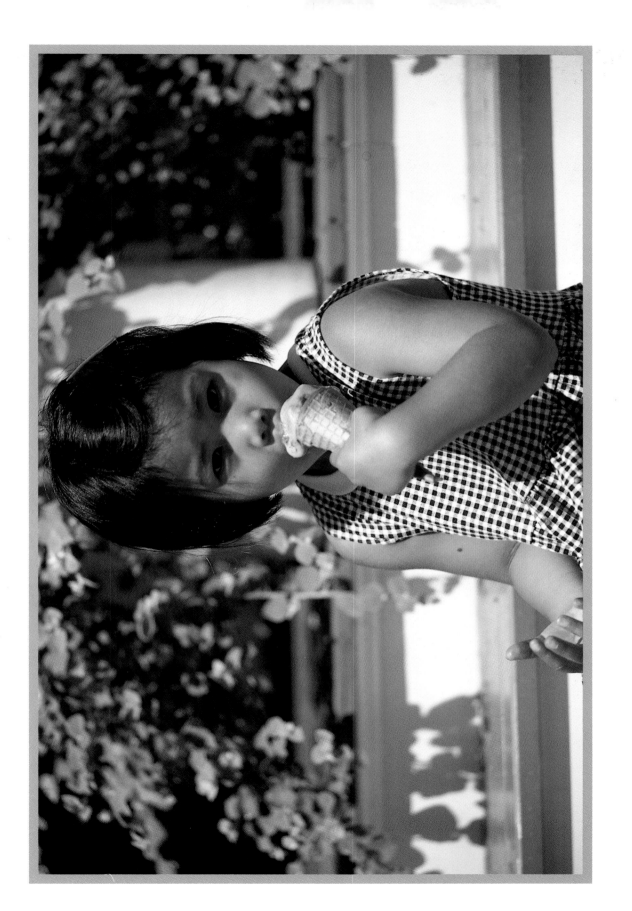

and ice cream.

With my ears I hear my baby brother,

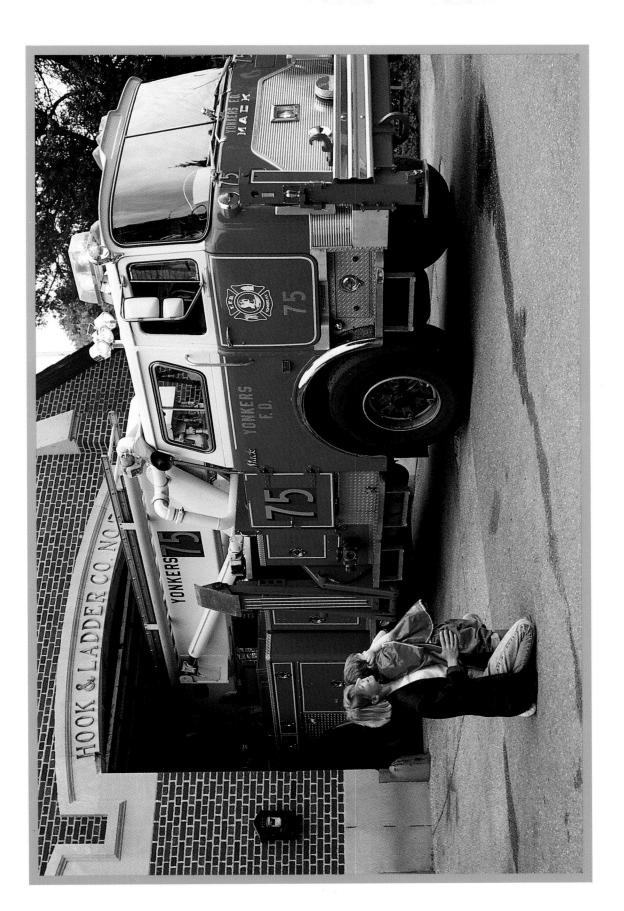

a fire engine,

my piano,

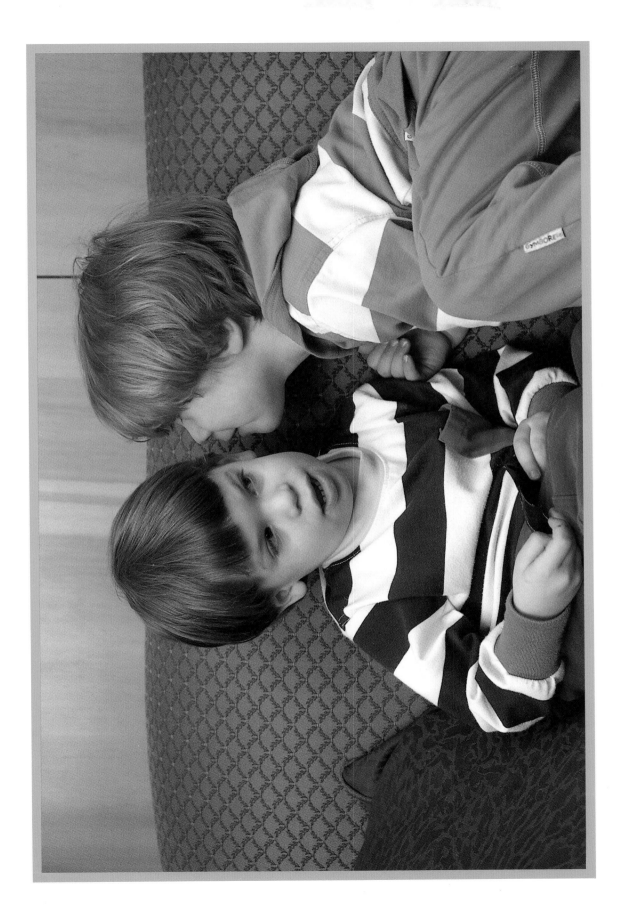

and whispered secrets.

With my hands I feel finger paints,

sand,

water,

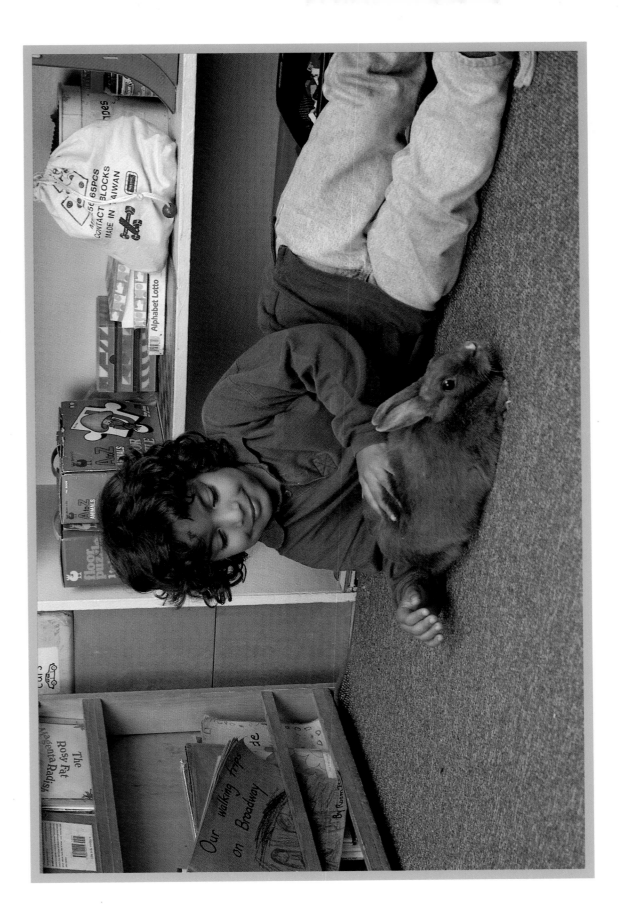

and a rabbit.

With our five senses, we enjoy our world.

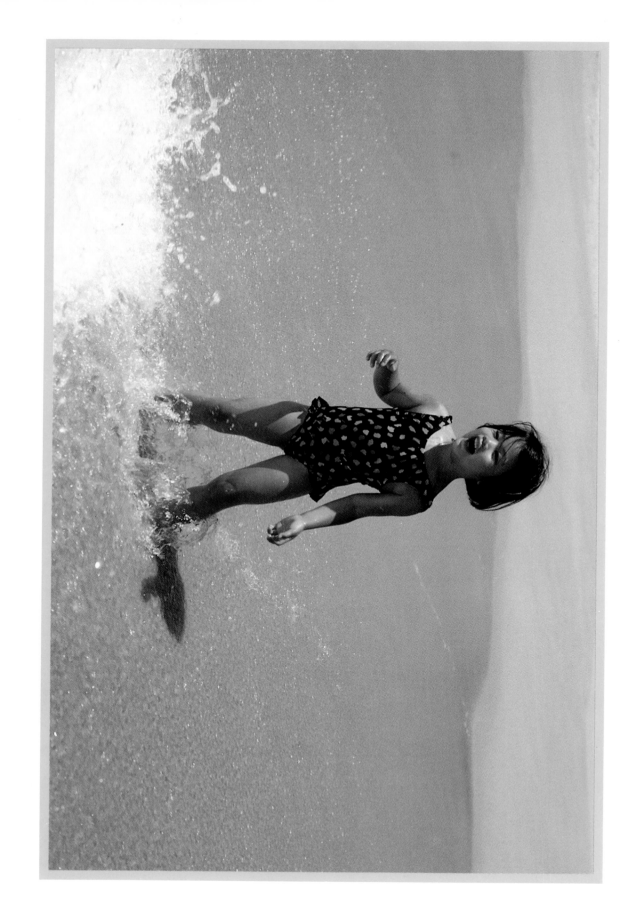